IT'S MY STATE!

MICHIGAN

Johannah Haney

Richard Hantula

Marshall Cavendish
Benchmark
New York

Library of Congress Cataloging-in-Publication Data
Haney, Johannah.
   Michigan / Johannah Haney and Richard Hantula.—2nd ed.
     p. cm. — (It's my state!)
   Includes bibliographical references and index.
   Summary: "Surveys the history, geography, government, economy, and people
   of Michigan"—Provided by publisher.
   ISBN 978-1-60870-523-8 (print) — ISBN 978-1-60870-701-0 (ebook)
   1. Michigan—Juvenile literature. I. Hantula, Richard. II. Title.
  F566.3.H36 2012
  977.4—dc22   2010046780

Second Edition developed for Marshall Cavendish Benchmark by RJF Publishing LLC (www.RJFpublishing.com)
Series Designer, Second Edition: Tammy West/Westgraphix LLC

All maps, illustrations, and graphics © Marshall Cavendish Corporation. Maps and artwork on pages 6, 28, 29, 75, 76, and back cover by Christopher Santoro. Map and graphics on pages 8 and 46 by Westgraphix LLC.

The photographs in this book are used by permission and through the courtesy of:
Front cover: IIene MacDonald/Alamy and Steve Skjold/Alamy (inset).
Alamy: John Glover, 4 (left); David Stuckel, 4 (right); Ross Frid, 5; Spring Images, 9; Jim West, 10, 18, 50, 54; David R. Frazier Photolibrary, Inc., 11; Eyecon Images, 12; Peter Arnold, Inc., 13, 16; Daniel Dempster Photography, 14; Corbis Flirt, 21; Steffen Hauser/botanikfoto, 22; Jennifer Brown, 23 (right); Buddy Mays, 23 (left); North Wind Picture Archives, 30, 31; Dennis MacDonald, 51, 56; Dennis Cox, 53; Cynthia Lindow, 55; Jess Merrill, 58, 60; Daniel Teetor, 65; IIene MacDonald, 69; Chris Raboir Sports Photography, 73; Universal Images Group Limited, 75 (top).
Artist Robert Griffing and Publisher, Paramount Press: 33. **Associated Press:** Jim Dufresne, 17; Paul Sancya, 44; Craig Porter, 74.
Getty Images: Archive Photos, 37, 41, 48; Bloomberg, 42; Getty Images News, 47; Getty Images Entertainment, 49 (right); Wally Eberhart, 70.
Milwaukee Public Museum: 24. **Superstock:** Indexstock, 27; Superstock, 36; Al Zwiazek, 39; Wolfgang Kaehler, 46, 62; Imagebroker.net, 49 (left), 63; Corbis, 52; George Ostertag, 64; F1 ONLINE, 71.

Every effort has been made to locate copyright holders of the images used in this book.

Printed in Malaysia (T).
135642

MICHIGAN

CONTENTS

THE WOLVERINE STATE

State Tree: White Pine

The white pine was named Michigan's official state tree in 1955. It can grow to heights of more than 100 feet (30 meters) and can have a trunk that is more than 4 feet (1.2 m) wide. This tree has become a symbol of lumbering, one of Michigan's greatest industries. White pines also serve as homes to various kinds of wildlife found in Michigan, including the majestic bald eagle.

State Bird: American Robin

Recognized by its dark coloring and red chest, the robin can be found all over Michigan—in backyards, gardens, fields, and forests. The birds nest in the spring and early summer, with females laying up to seven delicate blue eggs that hatch in about two weeks. The robin was made the official state bird in 1931.

State Flower: Apple Blossom

Flowering on the branches of apple trees, the apple blossom has large, pink-and-white petals and green leaves. It is very fragrant and has a sweet, pleasing smell. Apples are an important crop for the state, and this flower was officially chosen in 1897.

State Fish: Brook Trout

Brook trout thrive in the cold lakes, streams, and ponds of Michigan. In late summer or early fall, they lay their eggs on the gravel floor of small streams. They usually do not live longer than six years. Brook trout are a favorite catch for Michigan fishers. Michigan lawmakers in 1965 named the trout as the official state fish. Many different kinds of fish are called trout, however. In 1988, lawmakers specified the brook trout as the official fish.

State Reptile: Painted Turtle

In 1995, Michigan designated the painted turtle as its official state reptile. These reptiles can be found throughout the state. They can range in length from 5 inches to 10 inches (13 to 25 centimeters). Painted turtles have yellow or red markings on their dark skin and shells. They live in and near water, and their diet includes insects, plants, crayfish, and mollusks.

State Wildflower: Dwarf Lake Iris

This attractive plant, which has blue or violet flowers, was made the official state wildflower in 1998. Dwarf lake irises grow well in moist and sandy soil and are found along the shores of Lake Huron and Lake Michigan.

MICHIGAN

CANADA

Isle Royale

Isle Royale National Park

LAKE SUPERIOR

Mount Arvon

Marquette

L'Anse

Huron Mountains

Porcupine Mountains

Hiawatha National Forest

Escanaba River

Sault Sainte Marie

Bois Blanc Island

Cheboygan

Black Lake

Mallets Lake

Alpena

LAKE HURON

STRAITS OF MACKINAC

Beaver Island

Petoskey

Lake Charlevoix

Hubbard Lake

Traverse City

Higgins Lake

Houghton Lake

Cadillac

LAKE MICHIGAN

Manistee National Forest

Midland

Saginaw Bay

Saginaw

Muskegon River

Saginaw

Flint

Port Huron

Muskegon

Grand River

Grand Rapids

Lansing

Kalamazoo River

Lake St. Clair

Kalamazoo

Detroit

Ann Arbor

Battle Creek

LAKE ERIE

N

W E

S

The Wolverine State

Michigan is home to many bodies of fresh water. There are more than 11,000 lakes in Michigan, and streams flow for more than 36,000 miles (58,000 kilometers) within its borders. Michigan is the only state that borders four of the five Great Lakes. In fact, someone could stand anywhere in Michigan and be within 6 miles (10 km) of a lake or stream or within 85 miles (135 km) of one of the Great Lakes.

The Michigan landscape of today was shaped by a series of massive glaciers, or sheets of ice, that moved slowly across the land beginning more than 2 million years ago. As the glaciers—some as thick as a mile (1.6 km) or more—crept along, they carved out Michigan's geographical features. The Great Lakes and Michigan's valleys, rivers, hills, ridges, and flatlands are all mainly a result of glacial movement. The glaciers of the most recent glacial period began to melt about 14,000 years ago, leaving behind soil, pebbles, and boulders.

Michigan has a land area of 56,804 square miles (147,121 square kilometers), making it the twenty-second-largest state

Quick Facts

MICHIGAN BORDERS

North	Lake Superior
	Lake Huron
South	Indiana
	Ohio
East	Canada
	Lake Huron
	Lake Erie
West	Lake Michigan
	Wisconsin

Michigan has 83 counties.

in the United States in terms of land area. It has such a large water area—39,912 square miles (103,372 sq km)—that its total area is 96,716 square miles (250,493 sq km). It ranks as the eleventh-largest state in total area.

Michigan is made up of two peninsulas: the Upper Peninsula and the Lower Peninsula. Peninsulas are pieces of land that stick out into bodies of water. The state has a total of eighty-three counties in its two peninsulas.

The Upper Peninsula

Some have said that the Upper Peninsula is shaped like a rabbit. Most of this peninsula is made up of forests. Farms are spread out across the region. The cities of the Upper Peninsula generally have smaller populations than the ones in the Lower Peninsula. Marquette, located on Lake Superior, is the Upper Peninsula's most-populated city.

Scenic Lake of the Clouds is one of thousands of lakes that dot the Michigan landscape.

Quick Facts

HIGH POINT

Michigan's highest point is located in the Upper Peninsula. Mount Arvon, in Baraga County, is 1,979 feet (603 m) above sea level.

Sault Sainte Marie is another important city in the Upper Peninsula. Located in the east near the Canadian border, it is Michigan's oldest city. Because it sits on the shores of the Saint Mary's River—which connects Lake Huron and Lake Superior—Sault Sainte Marie has long been important to the state's economy.

In the northwestern section of the Upper Peninsula are the tree-covered Porcupine Mountains. The native Ojibwe, or Chippewa, people called the mountains "Kag-wadjiw," which means Porcupine Mountains, because they looked like a porcupine rising out of Lake Superior. The mountain range is 12 miles (19 km) long and is located in Ontonagon and Gogebic counties. State parks and skiing sites in the region are favorite spots for many Michiganders. Some residents refer to the Porcupine Mountains as simply "The Porkies."

The Upper Peninsula is also home to many national sites that are valued for their natural beauty. Pictured Rocks National Lakeshore is located on the

Isle Royale National Park is home to moose and many other kinds of wildlife.

peninsula's Lake Superior shore. Isle Royale National Park is a large island in the lake. Hiawatha National Forest, Seney National Wildlife Refuge, and Ottawa National Forest are also popular places for hikers, campers, and sightseers. Already open for use is much of the Upper Peninsula portion of the North Country National Scenic Trail, which is being assembled by the National Park Service in the northern United States. (Segments of the trail in the Lower Peninsula are also open.) The Keweenaw Peninsula, which juts out into Lake Superior, was once a major copper-mining

Quick Facts

ISLE ROYALE GREENSTONE

Isle Royale is the place where a beautiful greenish mineral called chlorastrolite was originally found. When bits of it began to be used in jewelry, they were sometimes referred to as Isle Royale greenstones. The mineral also occurs in the Keweenaw Peninsula. In 1972, it was named Michigan's official state gemstone.

area. Visitors to Keweenaw National Historical Park can learn about the area's heritage while enjoying its natural charms. The remote Harbor Island National Wildlife Refuge is located in Potagannissing Bay on Lake Huron.

The Lower Peninsula

The Upper and Lower peninsulas are connected only by a great human-made bridge that stretches over 5 miles (8 km) of water called the Straits of Mackinac. (The straits connect Lakes Michigan and Huron.) The Lower Peninsula is often described as being shaped like a mitten. The land is a mixture of forests, hills, flatlands, and sand dunes. Major cities in the Lower

Completed in 1957, the Mackinac Bridge, connecting the Upper and Lower peninsulas, is one of the longest suspension bridges in the world.

Peninsula include Detroit, Grand Rapids, Warren, Sterling Heights, Lansing, Ann Arbor, and Flint.

Detroit is Michigan's largest city. Located in the east, on the shore of the Detroit River, the city has played a key role in the state's history—in part because of its location near Canada and along the river that links Lake Saint Clair with Lake Erie.

Moving north or west from Detroit, other Michigan cities include Saginaw, Flint, Ann Arbor, and Jackson. Central portions of the state are home to cities such as Mount Pleasant and Lansing, Michigan's capital. West of Lansing are the large cities of Battle Creek, Grand Rapids, and Kalamazoo. The city with the biggest population on the Lower Peninsula's western coast is Muskegon.

Some of the Lower Peninsula's most famous natural features are its sand dunes. A sand dune is a ridge or hill made up of sand. The sand in these dunes consists mostly of the mineral quartz. Most of the sand was created when heavy glaciers passed over the area and crushed the rock into sand. The dunes formed as a result of the action of winds and moving water. The sand dunes in Michigan are considered to be one of the great wonders of the world, and Michigan has the world's largest group of freshwater sand dunes. Sand dunes are located along much of the shore of the Great Lakes, but the state's best-known dunes are on

Detroit's riverfront location helped it grow to become the largest city in Michigan.

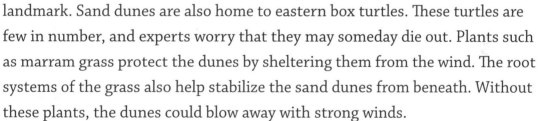
Some of Michigan's fragile dunes are protected in Sleeping Bear Sand Dunes National Lakeshore.

the Lake Michigan shore in the western part of the Lower Peninsula. There are more than 275,000 acres (111,000 hectares) of sand dunes in Michigan. The Sleeping Bear Sand Dunes National Lakeshore can even be seen from outer space. In open areas of the dunes, the surface temperature of the sand can be as hot as 120 to 180 degrees Fahrenheit (50 to 80 degrees Celsius).

The sand dunes are home to various kinds of plants and animals that might not be found in other parts of Michigan. Birds and insects migrating during the year use the dunes as a landmark. Sand dunes are also home to eastern box turtles. These turtles are few in number, and experts worry that they may someday die out. Plants such as marram grass protect the dunes by sheltering them from the wind. The root systems of the grass also help stabilize the sand dunes from beneath. Without these plants, the dunes could blow away with strong winds.

Sleeping Bear Sand Dunes National Lakeshore is one of many treasured natural sites in the Lower Peninsula. Others recognized by the federal government include Manistee National Forest, Huron National Forest, Thunder Bay National Marine Sanctuary and Underwater Preserve, Michigan Islands National Wildlife Refuge, and Shiawassee National Wildlife Refuge.

The Detroit River International Wildlife Refuge—the first international wildlife refuge in North America—is a joint effort between the United States and Canada. The refuge was established in 2001.

The majestic Upper Tahquamenon Falls are more than 200 feet (60 m) wide and have a drop of almost 50 feet (15 m).

The Great Lakes

The Great Lakes are a collection of five lakes: Lake Superior, Lake Michigan, Lake Huron, Lake Erie, and Lake Ontario. The only Great Lake that does not touch the borders of Michigan is Lake Ontario. The lakes have helped shape Michigan's shores, which feature many bays and coves. Michigan's land also includes islands surrounded by the lakes' waters.

Though Michigan may be famous for its location on the Great Lakes, the state also has many important inland bodies of water. The Upper Peninsula has rivers such as the Menominee, Whitefish, Manistique, Tahquamenon, and Escanaba. The Saint Joseph, Kalamazoo, Saginaw, Muskegon, and Au Sable rivers are just some of the large waterways crossing through parts of the Lower Peninsula. Michigan's longest river is the Grand River. It starts in the south-central part of the state and flows toward the west, eventually emptying into Lake Michigan. The rushing waters of many of the state's streams and rivers form striking waterfalls. There are nearly 200 named waterfalls within Michigan's borders, almost all of them in the Upper Peninsula. The Upper Tahquamenon Falls rank as one of the largest waterfalls east of the Mississippi River.

The Michigan Wetlands

Some of Michigan's best natural resources are its wetlands. Wetlands are areas of land close to water with a lot of moisture in the soil. Sometimes they may even be covered with shallow water. Examples of wetlands include swamps, bogs, and marshes. But Michigan wetlands are found especially often along the coasts of the Great Lakes. These are called coastal wetlands.

The wetlands provide a unique habitat for the plants and animals that thrive there. Flowers such as milkweed and boneset attract butterflies such as monarchs, swallowtails, and fritillaries. Chorus frogs and tree frogs make the wetlands their temporary homes while they raise their tadpoles. Tall grasses provide shade for insects and animals. Wetlands are also vital to ducks, geese, and other birds as they migrate. The wetlands provide water, food, and a place to rest as these birds fly south for the winter or north for the summer.

The Changing Seasons

Michigan's climate is affected by the Great Lakes. The winds from the water help cool temperatures in summer and keep them a little warmer in the winter. In the summer, temperatures usually range from about 50 °F to about 83 °F (10 to 28 °C). The Upper Peninsula usually experiences cooler temperatures than the Lower Peninsula. Michigan does not often suffer damaging summer storms, although tornadoes occasionally strike, especially in the southern part of the Lower Peninsula. On July 13, 1936, Michiganders in Mio suffered through the highest temperature ever recorded in the state: a blistering 112 °F (44 °C).

Many people especially enjoy Michigan in the fall. The temperatures are usually neither too cold nor too hot. And the leaves on many of the state's trees change colors to striking oranges, yellows, and reds. By November, however, snow starts to fall and temperatures begin to drop.

The winter months in Michigan are chilly, with temperatures usually between about 3 °F and 36 °F (between −16 °C and 2 °C). Michigan is one of several states on the Great Lakes that experience lake-effect snow. The water of the Great Lakes is often warmer than the air during the coldest months. When cold, dry arctic air passes over the lakes, the air is heated by the warmer water below. Water evaporates into the dry air, and large amounts of snow fall. This is referred to as lake-effect snow. In January 1982, 129.5 inches (328.9 cm)—more than 10 feet (3 m)—of snow fell on Copper Harbor near the tip of the Upper Peninsula's Keweenaw Peninsula. This is the most on record for any month at any weather station in the state. But most years are not like 1982, and most

A forest on the Keweenaw Peninsula is ablaze with the colors of autumn.

places in Michigan are not like Copper Harbor. The average annual amount of snow that falls in Michigan ranges from roughly 40 inches (100 cm) in the southeastern part of the Lower Peninsula to more than 200 inches (500 cm) in the Copper Harbor region. On February 9, 1934, Vanderbilt in Otsego County in the northern Lower Peninsula shivered through the lowest temperature that was ever recorded in Michigan: –51 °F (–46 °C).

After cold Michigan winters, spring is often a welcome time for residents. Temperatures begin to rise, but it is not uncommon to have snow in April. Spring in Michigan can be rainy and very wet. But the promise of summer helps keep many Michiganders in good spirits.

Wildlife

Michigan has a wide variety of plants, flowers, fish, and other wildlife. About 53 percent of the land in the state is covered with forests. Tall pines, firs, cedars, maples, oaks, and birches are among the trees growing in these forests. Other trees found across the state include hickory, elm, spruce, and aspen.

Hundreds of types of flowers grow in Michigan. Evening primrose, dense blazing star, pale coneflower, rosinweed, milkweed, and smooth aster are a few examples. Some plants, such as pale agoseris, are found only in a few areas. Pale agoseris usually occurs in grassy areas more common in the Great Plains of the west-central United States. But it also grows in the northern part of Michigan's Lower Peninsula, which has open grassy areas like those found in the Great Plains.

Michigan's forests are home to animals such as deer, snowshoe hares, ducks, woodchucks, coyotes, badgers, bald eagles, black bears, and bobcats. White-tailed

Trout, salmon, and other kinds of fish live in the Manistee River, making it a popular destination for people who enjoy fishing.

deer are found in every county, and in 1997 this deer was picked as the official state game mammal. (Game means animals that are hunted.) Moose and gray wolves (also called timber wolves) are found on Isle Royale and have also been seen in the forests of the Upper Peninsula mainland.

Michigan's animals also include bats, beavers, raccoons, skunks, and rabbits. Cougars, or mountain lions, are native to Michigan. Experts thought they disappeared from the area in the early 1900s. In recent years, however, people have found evidence, mainly in the Upper Peninsula, that there may still be a small number of cougars. The evidence includes cougar tracks and photos of animals that seem to be cougars.

The state's best-known nickname actually comes from an animal. Michigan is often called the Wolverine State. No one knows for sure where this nickname comes from. Until a wolverine was sighted near Ubly in 2004, the animal had not been seen in the region in about 200 years. Wolverines apparently never lived in the region in large numbers. Wolverines can grow to be as big as medium-sized dogs, but they have been known to fight larger mammals such as bears. The fierce wolverine is the mascot for the University of Michigan's sports teams.

Many different kinds of birds make their homes in Michigan's trees. These include eagles, falcons, owls, hummingbirds, wrens, sparrows, doves, and cardinals. Other Michigan birds live in the state's wetlands, sand dunes, or grasslands. Some of these birds are herons, egrets, and sandpipers. One of Michigan's most famous birds is the rare Kirtland's warbler. These birds nest in jack pine trees in a few Michigan counties and fly to the Bahama Islands or Caribbean islands for the winter. Some people think that the Kirtland's warbler should be made Michigan's state bird, replacing the robin, which is also the official bird of a few other states.

Michigan's waters are filled with fish, amphibians, and other water creatures. Frogs, toads, and salamanders live in Michigan's moist areas. Fish such as lake herring, carp, catfish, perch, bass, salmon, sturgeon, and muskellunge swim through the rivers, streams, and lakes.

Endangered Animals

An endangered species is a type of animal or plant that exists in such small numbers that it is in danger of becoming extinct and disappearing forever. Species may become endangered when their natural environment is damaged or destroyed as a result of natural disasters, human interference, or pollution. A species' continued existence may also be threatened by disease.

The Indiana bat is one endangered species found in Michigan. This mammal has grayish-brown fur and a pink underbelly. It is about 3 inches (7.6 cm) long and has a wingspan (the total length from one wingtip to the other when the wings are stretched out) of 9 to 11 inches (23 to 28 cm). These bats hibernate throughout the winter in caves or abandoned mines. During the spring and summer months, they live near streams, under loose bark in trees. Fewer than 400,000 of these bats remain in the United States. Federal law makes it illegal for humans to interfere with or harm in any way endangered species such as these little creatures.

Another endangered animal in Michigan is the Kirtland's warbler, a rare bird that usually mates in Michigan. Known for its loud song, it lives mostly in young jack pine trees in the northern parts of the Lower Peninsula. Jack pine trees depend on natural wildfires to destroy old trees, making room for young jack pines to grow. Since natural wildfires are being prevented—so that human communities will not be destroyed—the birds have fewer young jack pines in which to live. The warbler was placed on the endangered species list by the U.S. Fish and Wildlife Service in 1973. But efforts by scientists in Michigan and elsewhere to plant more young jack pines have led to an increase in the number of Kirtland's warblers.

Loss of habitat and overhunting caused the gray wolf to be classified as endangered. Efforts have since been made to preserve gray wolf populations. For example, it is illegal to harm a wolf unless you are protecting yourself. As a result, gray wolf populations have increased in Michigan and some other areas. However, at the beginning of 2011, Michigan wolves remained on the federal endangered species list.

Michiganders know that the preservation of their land and the plants and animals that live there is important. The Michigan Department of Natural Resources conserves and protects the state's natural resources by doing research to prevent problems, teaching residents about how to protect the environment, and taking action when a problem arises. By protecting the environment, Michiganders ensure their land will be healthy for future generations.

Endangered by hunting and loss of habitat, gray wolves in Michigan are making a comeback thanks to the efforts of conservationists.

Plants & Animals

Cardinal Flower

The cardinal flower is found along river and stream banks, along the shores of lakes, and in swamps. This plant's name comes from its ruby-red flowers. They bloom in late summer and early fall, and they often attract hummingbirds. The flowers have a soft, velvety texture. Cardinal flowers sometimes grow in large colonies along ditches in wet soil.

Four-Toed Salamander

The four-toed salamander can be found throughout most of Michigan in boggy ponds, creeks, and forests. These amphibians measure 2 to 4 four inches (5 to 10 cm) long, and they have just four toes on their hind feet. (Many other types of salamanders have five toes on their hind feet.) They eat insects, spiders, and worms. Four-toed salamanders hide under rotting logs and leaves.

Short-Eared Owl

Short-eared owls live in grasslands, and, unlike other kinds of owls, they hunt both during the day and at night. They nest in clumps of plants or at the base of shrubs in Michigan's grasslands. A typical nest might contain between five and seven eggs. When the eggs hatch, the young stay in the nest for just a couple of weeks before exploring the plants nearby.

Black Bear

Black bears are most common in the Upper Peninsula. A female bear comes out of her den in spring with her cubs, or baby bears. The cubs explore their new surroundings throughout the summer and early fall, eating nuts, insects, and berries. In late fall, the mother finds a den for herself and her cubs. They

remain there until the next spring, when the cubs go off on their own. Female black bears weigh between 100 and 250 pounds (between 45 and 113 kilograms), and adult males can weigh from 150 to 400 pounds (68 to 180 kg).

Jack Pine

Jack pines thrive in the drier parts of Michigan. Found on sand dunes and in regions with sandy soil, the trees are often short and tend to have a crooked trunk. Michigan's lumber industry harvests jack pines for use as building materials and for making paper.

Green Darner Dragonfly

The green darner dragonfly is one of the largest and most spectacular of all types, or species, of dragonfly. Green darners have silvery wings, a deep-emerald-colored throat, and a blue belly with a streak of deep red. They can be seen from spring through fall near bodies of water. Dragonflies eat smaller insects, sometimes picking them out of the air and eating them while still in flight.

From the Beginning

Around 12,000 BCE, the glaciers that once covered the region that is now Michigan began retreating. This process took many centuries. Scientists believe that humans first started living in the area roughly around 10,000 BCE. These early people are called Paleo-Indians ("ancient Indians"). They used stone tools and hunted animals with spears. They also gathered plants for food.

Copper People and Mound Builders

The period lasting from about 8000 BCE to about 1000 BCE is called the Archaic period. The peoples living then developed new tools using stone and wood. Large deposits of copper were found on Isle Royale and the Keweenaw Peninsula. Copper mining began. The people who made and used copper tools and other objects are sometimes called the Old Copper people. Things made of copper and other materials dating from the later parts of the Archaic period have been found in places other than where the materials originated. This suggests that trade activity was already going on at that time.

Many experts call the next period, beginning about 1000 BCE, the Woodland period. People in this period began planting gardens, making pottery, and building mounds of earth over graves. Sometime in the middle of the Woodland period, between around 300 BCE and around 500 CE, a new group of people

This museum display shows how ancient Indians may have mined copper thousands of years ago.

arrived from the south. Today many historians refer to this new group of people as the Hopewell.

The Hopewell people built very large burial mounds, some of which remain today. Along with their dead, the Hopewell buried items such as tools, pottery, and other goods. Enormous amounts of dirt were piled on top, forming the mounds. It is also possible that the mounds served some sort of religious purpose. As many as twenty people might be buried beneath a single mound. The Hopewell seem to have been great traders. Scientists have found in their mounds not only objects made of copper and other materials from the region but also objects using materials from very distant places—for example, shells from the Gulf of Mexico and freshwater pearls from the Mississippi River valley.

One of the best-known groups of Hopewell burial mounds is the Norton Mounds, in what is now Grand Rapids. Remains of pottery and tools found in the mounds are on display at the Van Andel Museum Center in Grand Rapids.

No one knows for sure what happened to the Hopewell people. They may have moved away or joined other groups of early peoples.

Three Fires

When the first Europeans arrived in the region in the early seventeenth century, three of the most important Indian groups in what is now Michigan were the Ojibwe, Ottawa (also called Odawa), and Potawatomi. These three groups were related. They had an alliance called the Council of Three Fires. The members of the three groups were known as the People of the Three Fires. They helped each other protect their land, and they shared hunting, farming, and craft skills.

The People of the Three Fires had some things in common. Most of them built canoes to travel on rivers and lakes, and some of them farmed to have a constant food source. Many of these people made snowshoes to wear in the winter and made nets for fishing. Some of them were skilled at weaving cloth to make clothes. As they interacted with other Indians and eventually with Europeans, the Ojibwe, Ottawa, and Potawatomi also began to use items such as beads, tobacco, musical instruments, and cooking pots.

Tents like this one were used by the Ojibwe people.

But even though they were similar to each other, the Ojibwe, Ottawa, and Potawatomi each had unique aspects to their cultures. For example, the Ottawa relied more heavily on trading. In fact their name comes from a word meaning "to trade."

The Hurons were another Indian group in the region that now includes Michigan. They lived in longhouses. They grew beans, corn, and squash and also hunted and fished. Their population before the Europeans arrived was estimated at about 30,000. By 1640, they were thought to number fewer than 10,000—as a result of disease and war.

MAKING A MEDICINE BAG

Some American Indians carried bags that held special leaves, flowers, roots, and pieces of bark that were used in treating illnesses and wounds. Many of the plants used were very common, such as daisies, primrose, wild mint, and beech, birch, and red oak trees. Following these instructions, you can make your own medicine bag.

WHAT YOU NEED

Brown felt—a piece at least as big as a rectangle
  of about 5 inches (12$\frac{1}{2}$ cm) by 10 inches (25 cm)

Scissors

Brown thread

A sewing needle with an eye—or hole—large
  enough for your thread

18 inches (45 cm) of ribbon or lacing

A few beads, with holes large enough for the ribbon

A small bundle of dried flowers or leaves

Measure your felt and cut it into a rectangle that is 5 inches (12$\frac{1}{2}$ cm) by 10 inches (25 cm). Fold the rectangle in half to make a 5-inch square.

Cut two pieces of thread—each piece should be 12 inches (30 cm) long. Thread the needle with one piece of thread and tie a small knot at the other end of the thread. The needle is sharp, so be very careful. You can have an adult help you thread the needle and sew.

Position the folded felt so that the folded edge is closest to you. Begin sewing the edge of the felt from the bottom toward the top opening. Once you reach the opening, sew stitches back toward you. When you reach the fold, tie a knot, and trim the extra thread. Repeat this sewing process for the other end of the felt.

Fold down the top of the bag (the opening) about 1 inch to $1\frac{1}{2}$ inches (roughly 3 cm). Using the scissors, make six slits along the fold. Each slit should be about $\frac{1}{2}$ inch (roughly 1 cm) long. Unfold the top. Thread the ribbon or lacing over and under the slits you have just made.

String some beads on each end of the ribbon or lacing and tie a knot at each end.

By pulling the lacing you can tighten and close your bag. Have fun finding and filling your medicine bag with flowers, leaves, or other small items.

The French Arrive

The first Europeans to reach what is now Michigan were the French. They began coming to the area in the early seventeenth century as they looked for a so-called Northwest Passage. This was a waterway that, it was thought, would cut across all of North America, making it possible to travel to Asia. In 1618, the French explorer Etienne Brûlé landed at what is now Sault Sainte Marie. He is believed to be the first European to set foot in the area we call Michigan. No waterway such as the Northwest Passage existed, but French traders kept returning to the area. They wanted the pelts—or fur—of fox, mink, and beaver. These pelts were very valuable in Europe and were used to make warm clothing and hats.

In this illustration, American Indians are shown bringing their furs to European traders.

By 1650, a number of French fur traders had traveled up the Saint Lawrence River to the Great Lakes to trade goods for furs from the American Indians. The French traded a variety of European goods for the fur pelts: cloth, iron pots, hatchets, guns, and alcohol. In the beginning, American Indians welcomed fur traders and taught them to speak their native languages and to track animals. French authorities wanted to control the trade, but many traders, called *coureurs de bois* ("runners of the woods"), went out into the forests on their own, without permission. Toward the end of the seventeenth century, some of these *coureurs de bois* began receiving official permission to do their work. They were referred to as *voyageurs* ("travelers"). They became famous for traveling the area's many rivers, streams, and lakes in canoes. But these Europeans still depended on Indian groups such as the Ottawa to help them get the furs.

As time went on, the European demand for furs soared. The Indians continued to supply the furs and came to rely on the Europeans for supplies. Many Indians stopped practicing traditional ways of life and worked only as trappers for the fur trade.

French Catholic missionaries also began coming to the area in the seventeenth century. Missionaries are people who travel to spread their beliefs and way of life. The most famous French missionary in the region was Jacques Marquette. Marquette is also considered one of the great explorers of North America. He arrived in Quebec, Canada, in 1666. There he worked among the Indians, learning some of their languages and teaching them about Christianity. In 1668, Marquette founded a mission at a place that was given the name Sault Sainte Marie. This is considered the first European settlement in the land that now makes up Michigan.

In 1671, Marquette established the St. Ignace mission on the north shore of the Straits of Mackinac between the Upper and

In Their Own Words

On the 17th day of May 1673, we started from the mission of St. Ignace at Michilimackinac.... The joy that we felt at being selected for this expedition animated our courage. ...We obtained all the information that we could from the [Indians] who had frequented those regions; and we even traced out from their reports a map of that new country.

—From the travel notes of Father Jacques Marquette

Explorer and missionary Jacques Marquette met with Indian peoples in what is now Michigan beginning in the 1660s.

Lower peninsulas. The region's first French military fort, Fort De Baude, was built at St. Ignace around 1690. Traders called the outpost Michilimackinac, the Ojibwe name for the area. The fort was manned for only a few years. In 1715, a new fort called Fort Michilimackinac was built on the northern tip of the Lower Peninsula. It became a busy fur-trading center.

An important role in the region was played by an officer named Antoine Laumet de la Mothe, sieur de Cadillac. In 1694, he took command of Fort De Baude. Cadillac later decided that the French needed to build another post farther south, to protect the area against the English, who had already colonized much of North America's east coast. Cadillac proposed building the new fort on the waterway between Lakes Huron and Erie. The French called this waterway Détroit ("The Strait"). The French king, Louis XIV, agreed, and in 1701, Cadillac and about one hundred people founded Fort Ponchartrain. The settlement at Fort Ponchartrain would one day become the city of Detroit. The portion of the waterway by Detroit is now called the Detroit River.

The British Take Control

Until the eighteenth century, the French had the only European settlements in the region. But the profits from the fur trade made the British interested in the area. In 1754, war broke out in North America between France and Great Britain. The fighting spread to Europe in 1756 and then to other parts of the world. In North America, where the struggle is often referred to as the French and Indian War (1754–1763), Britain and France fought over who would control what is now the Midwest and parts of Canada, including

Quick Facts

FAME FOREVER
The names of some of Michigan's cities honor famous people. Cadillac was named after the French officer Antoine Laumet de la Mothe, sieur de Cadillac. Marquette was named for the French missionary and explorer Jacques Marquette. Pontiac carries the name of the Indian leader Pontiac.

the land that makes up Michigan. The war ended with a British victory in 1763, and as a result, most of North America east of the Mississippi River officially came under British control. Formerly French forts were now occupied by British soldiers, and more land was being settled by the British.

In this painting, Ojibwe warriors are shown planning an attack on a British fort during the conflict that became known as Pontiac's Rebellion.

During the French and Indian War, most of the fighting in North America had ended by 1760. As the British took over, some Indian leaders, including an Ottawa chief called Pontiac, felt that the time had come when the Europeans' presence and their interference with Indian cultures could no longer be tolerated. The Indians feared the loss of their hunting grounds to British settlers. There were other complaints as well. The British paid less for furs than the French had paid, and when the Indians came to the forts to trade, they found themselves less welcome than before. Moreover, the British were no longer willing to promote good relations by supplying the Indians with food, guns, and clothing. Pontiac gathered together a number of Indians from the Great Lakes area and planned a surprise attack against the British. This would later be called Pontiac's Rebellion.

In May 1763, Pontiac and his warriors surrounded and attacked the British fort at Detroit, and other Indian warriors began attacking forts and outposts elsewhere in the region. The Indians succeeded in capturing several British forts, but Detroit remained in British control for nearly seven months. Eventually, Pontiac and his men were forced to give up. Their siege of Detroit was the last major confrontation between Indians and European settlers in what is now Michigan.

After the French and Indian War, Britain needed money to pay for the costs of war. The British government sought to impose new taxes on the people in its American colonies. Hoping to avoid new conflicts with the Indians, Britain tried to stop the colonists from settling in much of the region it took over from France. The British government also set up other rules and laws that the colonists did not like. These actions led many colonists to want independence from Britain and eventually contributed to the outbreak of the American Revolution in 1775.

A New Nation

Most of the fighting of the American Revolution (1775–1783) took place on the east coast of North America. To help keep their position in what is now Michigan, the British abandoned the wooden Fort Michilimackinac on the south shore of the Straits of Mackinac and built a strong new stone fort on Mackinac Island, located in Lake Huron just outside the straits. This fort, called Fort Mackinac, was built around 1780. In 1783, the Americans won the war, and the Treaty of Paris was signed. According to the treaty, the Americans gained control of the land that would become Michigan. But the British did not actually surrender Fort Mackinac until 1796.

In 1787, Congress—the governing body of the now-independent United States—passed a law organizing the large area northwest of the Ohio River that

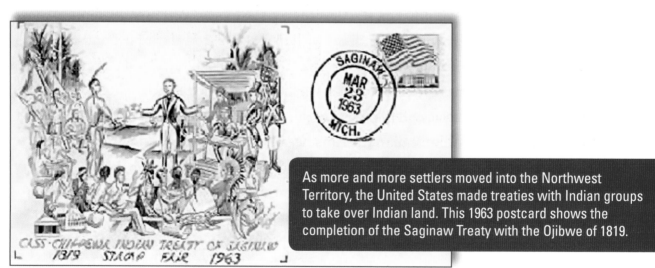

As more and more settlers moved into the Northwest Territory, the United States made treaties with Indian groups to take over Indian land. This 1963 postcard shows the completion of the Saginaw Treaty with the Ojibwe of 1819.

had been received from Britain. This area—called the Northwest Territory—would eventually become the states of Michigan, Ohio, Indiana, Illinois, and Wisconsin, as well as part of Minnesota. The law was called the Northwest Ordinance. It said that a region within the Northwest Territory could apply for statehood once its population reached sixty thousand. In 1805, Congress established the Territory of Michigan, which included present-day Michigan along with Wisconsin and part of Minnesota. But it would still be many years before Michigan was eligible for statehood.

The new United States struggled against the British one more time during the War of 1812. The Americans were angry because the British often kidnapped American sailors and made them work on British ships. These kidnappings were called impressments. The Americans also discovered that the British were supplying Indian groups with weapons and encouraging them to attack American settlements. In the early stages of the war, the British quickly captured Fort Mackinac and Detroit, and for a year or so, they controlled Michigan again. But the American navy achieved an important victory on Lake Erie in 1813. The Battle of Lake Erie forced the British out of the Michigan Territory for good.

Michigan Becomes a State

Many people began to settle in the Michigan Territory in the early nineteenth century. The Erie Canal was completed in New York State in 1825. It linked the Great Lakes with the Atlantic Ocean. This waterway provided a quick and easy route between the eastern states and the lands of the old Northwest Territory. Transporting goods and people to Michigan no longer required a long

Quick Facts

LAKE LAND
The name *Michigan* comes from a French version of the Ojibwe word *michi-gama*, which means "big lake." The French used the word to refer to the lake now known as Lake Michigan. The name was first officially applied to a land area in 1805, when Congress established the Territory of Michigan.

and difficult trip overland. This helped draw settlers to the fertile farmland that Michigan provided. The Michigan Territory's population grew quickly, rising from roughly 9,000 in 1820 to 32,000 in 1830.

A special census found in 1834 that some 86,000 people were living in the Lower Peninsula—more than enough to apply for statehood. Michigan asked to become a state, with its boundaries to include mostly the Lower Peninsula. However, action on statehood was delayed by a conflict over a piece of land called the Toledo Strip. Both Michigan and Ohio claimed this narrow piece of land, which ran along their border from Indiana to Lake Erie. Both Michigan and Ohio sent soldiers to the area. The "Toledo War" ended without serious bloodshed. Congress decided that Ohio would win the Toledo Strip and that Michigan would be granted statehood if it accepted, in exchange, all of the Upper Peninsula. Michigan agreed, and on January 26, 1837, it became the twenty-sixth state to join the Union (another name for the United States). Detroit served as its capital.

At first, Michiganders were insulted by the outcome of the conflict with Ohio. They felt that the Upper Peninsula was a poor trade for the port of Toledo, with its location on Lake Erie. But the Upper Peninsula provided Michigan with the natural resources that later in the century made it the nation's leader in copper, salt, and iron mining and in lumber production. These industries helped Michigan to prosper and attract many new residents. In 1847, the capital was moved to Lansing, which is located closer to the center of the state.

The first state election in Michigan after it was admitted to the Union was held in 1837.

Michigan in the Civil War

In 1861, the Civil War began in the United States. Michigan was one of almost two dozen states, most of them in the northern part of the nation, that sided with the federal government, also referred to as the Union. On the other side were eleven Southern states that seceded (withdrew) from the federal authority of the United States of America and formed the Confederate States of America. One of the issues that divided North and South was slavery. By the beginning of the 1860s, slavery was against the law in most of the North. In the South, there were millions of black slaves, many of them forced to work on the region's plantations (large farms).

An escaped slave herself, Sojourner Truth helped many slaves traveling through Michigan to freedom in Canada.

Slavery was always against the law in the state of Michigan. Antislavery groups, which wanted to see slavery ended throughout the United States, had begun forming in Michigan in the 1830s. Many Michiganders played an important role in helping slaves from the South escape to freedom. A large number of these slaves traveled through Michigan to Canada, where slavery was banned and escaped slaves could not be captured and returned. Abolitionists, people who were against slavery, hid the escaping slaves and provided food, shelter, and money as the slaves journeyed north. This network of homes, churches, barns, stores, and schools was called the Underground Railroad. A woman from Adrian, Michigan, named Laura Haviland helped so many slaves that she came to be known as the Superintendent of the Underground Railroad. Another key figure in the Underground Railroad was Sojourner Truth, a former slave who moved to the Battle Creek area in the late 1850s. Detroit, Adrian, and Battle Creek were among the stops on the Underground Railroad.

More than ninety thousand men from Michigan served on the side of the Union in the Civil War, including more than 1,600 African Americans and more than 200 Indians. Women from Michigan played an important role as well. The Michigan Soldier Relief Association was a group of Michigan women who provided medical care, clothing, food, and newspapers to wounded Michigan soldiers at hospitals in Washington, D.C. Historians believe that about fourteen thousand Michigan soldiers died during the war, either in battle or from disease. President Abraham Lincoln acknowledged the contribution Michiganders made to the war, declaring, "Thank God for Michigan."

The Civil War ended in a Union victory in 1865. The eleven states that had seceded were returned to the Union, and the Thirteenth Amendment to the U.S. Constitution prohibited slavery throughout the United States.

In Their Own Words

Michigan is loyal to the Union, the Constitution, and the laws, and will defend them to the uttermost; and to proffer to the president of the United States, the whole military power of the State for that purpose. . . . Let us abide in the faith of our fathers—"Liberty and Union, one and inseparable, now and forever."

—Michigan Governor Austin Blair, speaking to the Michigan legislature in 1861

Michigan's Industry and the Automobile

After the Civil War, Michigan prospered. The state's enormous supply of trees and minerals helped make it an ideal place to develop different industries. Michigan resources were used to provide the world with steel, ships, iron, stoves, and medicine. All this industry meant there were plenty of jobs in Michigan. Because of this, Michigan's population continued to grow. The population went from one million in 1870 to more than two million in 1890.

In the following years, pioneering automakers such as Ransom Olds and Henry Ford made Michigan the leader of the country's car industry. Olds, helped by Frank

The 1902 Oldsmobile was steered by using the tiller, or rod, at the front of the car, not with a steering wheel.

Clark, built an early gasoline-powered automobile in 1896 in Lansing. The following year, the Olds Motor Vehicle Company was formed. It made only a few cars, but it was succeeded in 1899 by the Olds Motor Works. At the time, most people thought that the idea of automobiles was crazy. The first automobiles were expensive and did not sell very well. Nonetheless, Olds's company managed to sell 600 cars in 1901. Three years later, the figure rose to 5,000. This marked the beginning of mass production of gasoline cars in the United States.

Henry Ford, who was born near Detroit, also built a gasoline-powered vehicle in 1896. His first attempts to form a company to make automobiles did not go well, but he eventually became even more successful than Olds at the mass production of automobiles. At the Ford Motor Company, formed in 1903, he adopted on a large scale the use of an assembly-line system, in which each employee puts together one piece of each car. Olds had introduced the assembly line into car manufacturing, but Ford expanded it and improved on it. Ford's assembly-line system sped up the construction of automobiles, and this reduced the price of the cars. In 1908, Ford's Model T cost $850, which was low compared to other cars of the time. By 1927, Ford had reduced the cost of the Model T to $380. Detroit quickly became the center of the automobile industry.

The Great Depression and Labor Movements

By 1929, Michigan's economy was based on the manufacturing of goods such as cars, refrigerators, and airplanes. But beginning late that year, the United States entered a period of severe economic hardship known as the Great Depression. Many businesses closed, and many people lost their jobs. Like other states,

Michigan was hit hard by these economic troubles. With millions of people out of work, the need for Michigan's manufactured items decreased—many people could no longer afford to buy them. By 1933, 46 percent of Michigan's workforce was jobless. By 1935, Michigan's population was down by nearly 30 percent since 1930, as people left the state to try to find jobs elsewhere.

The men and women who were able to keep their jobs often had to work long hours for low wages doing tiresome tasks. Workers formed unions—groups of employees who join together to try to obtain better pay and working conditions. In the 1930s, workers at automobile factories went on strike to protest the poor working conditions. Sometimes these strikes became violent. The nation's first large-scale "sit-down strike" took place in Flint at a General Motors Company factory. Bosses at General Motors refused to talk with the workers' union leaders, so the workers came to work and then sat down, not only refusing to work, but also refusing to leave the factory. The strike began at the end of 1936 and lasted 44 days. The workers were victorious. In 1937, General Motors recognized the workers' union, the United Auto Workers (UAW). This meant that General Motors would negotiate with the union about such matters as pay levels and working conditions. The other automobile manufacturers eventually followed the example of General Motors, and working conditions in the industry improved.

During the Great Depression, Michigan's economy was helped by President Franklin D. Roosevelt's New Deal programs. Under the New Deal, the federal government helped to create jobs and improve conditions around the country through such agencies as the Works Progress Administration (WPA) and the Civilian Conservation Corps (CCC). The WPA gave work to the unemployed constructing roads, buildings, bridges, and airports, creating parks, and doing a variety of other jobs. Under the CCC, the unemployed worked on state and federal land, planting trees, fighting forest fires, and building nature trails.

Michigan in World War II

Michigan's economy continued to recover with the onset of World War II (1939–1945). When the United States entered the war in 1941, products from

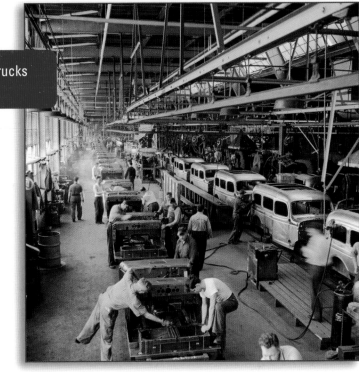

Workers at this Detroit auto plant build trucks for the army during World War II.

Michigan's factories were once again in high demand. Auto plants were converted to produce tanks, planes, naval vessels, trucks, and armored cars. Many of the factories that were closed down in the 1930s reopened and ran twenty-four hours a day, providing new jobs for many Michiganders.

Women again played an important role in the war efforts. With so many men serving in the armed forces, more and more women began working in factories in order to meet the demand for war supplies. To help popularize the idea of women working in factories, the federal government conducted an advertising campaign using the name "Rosie the Riveter," from a popular 1942 song. Rose Monroe, who worked in a factory in Ypsilanti, Michigan, was picked to star in a promotional film for the campaign. Her job included riveting—or connecting—parts for airplanes. Rosie the Riveter became a symbol of women's efforts on the home front during the war.

Modern Michigan

In general, the 1960s and 1970s were troubled times for Michigan. Its economy suffered once again as its automobile industry was hurt by increasing sales of cars from foreign automakers and by gasoline shortages.

Throughout most of Michigan's history, many African Americans in the state had very difficult lives. Even though the state, beginning in 1885, adopted several laws banning racial discrimination, African Americans still did not have the same rights and privileges as white people. African-American children often went to

As Michigan's auto industry recovered in 2010, President Barack Obama visited a Chrysler plant in Detroit.

separate schools from white children. Michigan felt the tension as the civil rights movement swept across the United States in the 1950s and 1960s. The civil rights movement fought for equal rights for everybody, regardless of race. As the entire country was struggling with the issue of race, many people worked together to find ways to bring about change. But some people opposed change, and some were angry that change was not occurring faster. There were race riots in several United States cities, including Detroit.

Economic difficulties continued in Michigan into the 1980s, but the 1990s showed more promise. Difficult times returned with a national economic slump early in the first decade of the twenty-first century. Another, more serious downturn began toward the end of the decade, when a financial crisis swept around the world. Michigan, with its big automotive industry, was especially hard hit. In 2009, Chrysler and General Motors even filed for reorganization under bankruptcy law. In the same year, Michigan's average unemployment rate reached 13.6 percent, at that time the highest level of any state in the country.

Still, the state has strong economic potential. By 2010, there were signs that auto companies were starting to do better financially. Besides auto firms, many large companies have their headquarters in Michigan. For example, the Dow Chemical Company, one of the largest chemical companies in the world, is based in Midland. These companies continue to provide many jobs for Michiganders.

Important Dates

★ **10,000** BCE Paleo-Indians arrive in the region.

★ **300** BCE The Hopewell people hunt and farm in the area.

★ **1618** French explorer Etienne Brûlé lands at the future site of Sault Sainte Marie, becoming the first European to set foot in what is now Michigan.

★ **1668** French missionary Jacques Marquette establishes the area's first European outpost, at Sault Sainte Marie.

★ **1701** Detroit is founded by Antoine Laumet de la Mothe, sieur de Cadillac.

★ **1783** The land that is now Michigan becomes part of the United States as a result of the treaty ending the American Revolution.

★ **1805** The Michigan Territory is created, with Detroit as its capital.

★ **1812** In the War of 1812, Fort Mackinac and Detroit are surrendered to the British.

★ **1813** American troops regain control of Detroit; the British leave Fort Mackinac in 1815.

★ **1837** President Andrew Jackson signs the bill making Michigan the nation's twenty-sixth state.

★ **1899** Ransom Olds of Lansing opens the first company to make gasoline-powered automobiles on a large scale.

★ **1908** Henry Ford's Model T goes into production.

★ **1935** The United Auto Workers Union is formed.

★ **1957** The Mackinac Bridge, connecting the Lower and Upper peninsulas, is completed.

★ **1974** Gerald Ford, a former Michigan congressman who had been appointed U.S. vice president the preceding year, becomes president.

★ **1987** Singer Aretha Franklin, who grew up in Detroit, is the first female inducted into the Rock and Roll Hall of Fame.

★ **2003** Jennifer M. Granholm becomes Michigan's first female governor.

★ **2010** Michigan auto companies begin to recover from economic hard times.

The People

Every ten years, the U.S. Census Bureau counts the number of people in the United States. According to the 2010 Census, 9,883,640 people were living in Michigan as of April 1 of that year. Michigan ranked eighth in the United States for highest population. Many people in Michigan live in cities, and almost half of the residents of Michigan live in the Detroit and Ann Arbor areas.

Where did all these people come from? According to a 2008 estimate by the Census Bureau, almost 583,000 Michiganders were born in a foreign country. But that is less than 6 percent of the population. The remaining Michiganders include people born elsewhere in the United States and people born in Michigan whose parents, grandparents, or other ancestors arrived in the region in the past. Many Michiganders can trace their roots to Britain or France. Others trace their heritage to such countries as Germany, Poland, and Ireland.

Quick Facts

MORE THAN ONE NAME
People who live in or come from Michigan may refer to themselves by different names. Some say "Michiganders," and some say "Michiganians." There are also people who say "Michiganites." Some residents of the Upper Peninsula, or the U.P., refer to themselves as "Yoopers."

The Bavarian Festival in Frankenmuth celebrates the cultural heritage of people of German descent.

Some cities in Michigan have a higher concentration of people from a certain part of the world. For instance, Dutch immigrants settled Holland, Michigan, in 1847. Every May, the people of Holland, Michigan, celebrate their Dutch heritage with Holland's Tulip Time Festival. Some neighborhoods in large cities, such as Greektown in Detroit, are made up largely of people of a certain ethnicity, with traditional ethnic grocery stores, bakeries, and festivals.

Many restaurants in Detroit's Greektown feature traditional Greek dishes.

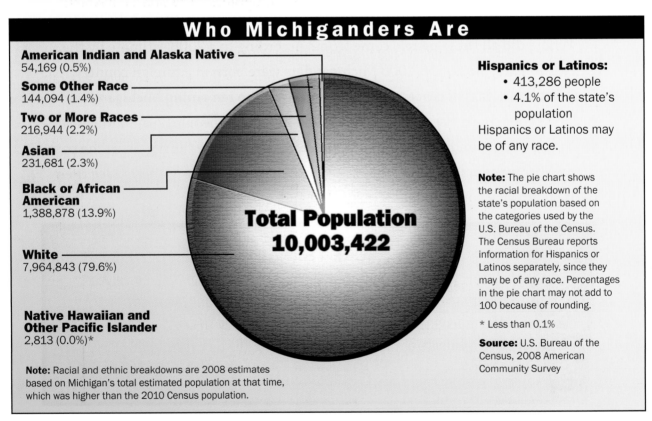

Who Michiganders Are

American Indian and Alaska Native
54,169 (0.5%)

Some Other Race
144,094 (1.4%)

Two or More Races
216,944 (2.2%)

Asian
231,681 (2.3%)

Black or African American
1,388,878 (13.9%)

White
7,964,843 (79.6%)

Native Hawaiian and Other Pacific Islander
2,813 (0.0%)*

**Total Population
10,003,422**

Hispanics or Latinos:
- 413,286 people
- 4.1% of the state's population

Hispanics or Latinos may be of any race.

Note: The pie chart shows the racial breakdown of the state's population based on the categories used by the U.S. Bureau of the Census. The Census Bureau reports information for Hispanics or Latinos separately, since they may be of any race. Percentages in the pie chart may not add to 100 because of rounding.

* Less than 0.1%

Source: U.S. Bureau of the Census, 2008 American Community Survey

Note: Racial and ethnic breakdowns are 2008 estimates based on Michigan's total estimated population at that time, which was higher than the 2010 Census population.

Michigan's large population is diverse. The largest minority group in Michigan is made up of African Americans, who represent about 14 percent of the population. Asian Americans make up slightly more than 2 percent. Nearly 80 percent of the population is white. Almost 55,000 American Indians live in Michigan. People of Hispanic descent (who may be of any race) make up slightly more than 4 percent of the population.

Arab Americans in Michigan

Michigan is home to the second-highest number of Arab Americans of any state in the country, after California. A 2008 estimate by the Census Bureau put the number of Arab Americans in Michigan at more than 150,000. Wayne County, Oakland County, and Macomb County—all in the greater Detroit area—have the highest number of Arab Americans in Michigan. Arab Americans account for two-fifths of the more than 100,000 residents of Dearborn, in Wayne County. Many of the Arab Americans in Michigan are immigrants from Middle Eastern countries. Others belong to families who have lived in the state for many years.

Like other state residents, Arab Americans in Michigan play an active role in the economy, the government, and other areas of daily life. For example, the Arab American Women's Business Council is an organization in Dearborn that helps women of Arab descent develop their business or professional careers. Organizations such as the American-Arab Anti-Discrimination Committee, a national group that has an office in Dearborn, help combat discrimination and hate crimes against Arab Americans.

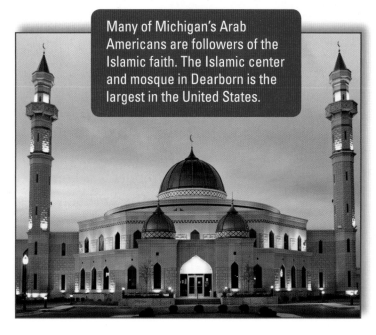

Many of Michigan's Arab Americans are followers of the Islamic faith. The Islamic center and mosque in Dearborn is the largest in the United States.

Famous Michiganders

William E. Boeing: Inventor and Businessman

William E. Boeing was born in Detroit in 1881. As an adult, he founded the Boeing Airplane Company, which made small planes. Today, Boeing is one of the world's largest aerospace companies. The company had already started making jet planes by the time Boeing died in 1956.

Charles Lindbergh: Aviator

The first person to make a nonstop solo flight across the Atlantic Ocean, Charles Lindbergh was born in Detroit in 1902. In 1927, Lindbergh flew 3,600 miles (5,800 km) in 33.5 hours from New York to Paris. He received the Congressional Medal of Honor and the Distinguished Flying Cross from President Calvin Coolidge. After his transatlantic flight, Lindbergh flew on a national tour, visiting 92 U.S. cities. He died in 1974 on the Hawaiian island of Maui.

Stevie Wonder: Musician

Stevie Wonder was born Steveland Judkins in Saginaw, Michigan, in 1950. He became blind shortly after birth. Despite his blindness, he was playing piano by age seven and later joined a church choir. When recording company Motown Records signed Steveland to a record contract, the company called him "Little Stevie Wonder." Later, the "Little" was dropped. Wonder has had numerous hit songs and has won more than twenty Grammy Awards. He is also known as a supporter of African-American rights.

Madonna: Singer, Songwriter, and Actress

Madonna was born Madonna Louise Veronica Ciccone in Bay City, Michigan, in 1958. She got a dance scholarship to the University of Michigan but left before graduating to try to make a career as a dancer in New York. She went on to become a superstar as a singer and has also appeared in movies. Madonna ranks as the top-selling female recording artist in history, according to *Guinness World Records*. In 2008, she was inducted into the Rock and Roll Hall of Fame.

Larry Page: Computer Scientist and Business Leader

Larry Page was born in Lansing, Michigan, in 1973, the son of a computer science professor and a computer programming teacher. While studying computer science at the University of Michigan, he built an inkjet printer out of Lego bricks. He went to Stanford University in California for graduate school. There he met fellow student Sergey Brin, and the two began developing an Internet search project they called BackRub. In 1998, they founded Google Inc., which soon expanded into a large multinational corporation. As of 2010, Page ranked as one of the world's richest billionaires.

Serena Williams: Tennis Player

Serena Williams was born in Saginaw in 1981. She entered her first tennis tournament when she was just four years old. Williams won the Olympic gold medal for women's doubles tennis in 2000 and 2008 with her sister, Venus. On the tennis tour, Williams has won many doubles titles and even more singles titles. In 2009, she broke the record for most prize money won by a female athlete in a career.

Diversity

Before the Civil War, many African Americans came to Michigan on the Underground Railroad to escape slavery. During World War II, African Americans were recruited from the South to work in Michigan's automobile plants. Today, nearly 1,400,000 African Americans live in Michigan. Of these, almost half—roughly 650,000—live in Detroit. African Americans in Michigan work in every field, including politics, industry, farming, medicine, and education. In 2001, the first Black Chamber of Commerce in Michigan opened its doors in Detroit, with a goal to provide support to African-American businesspeople.

Hispanic Americans and Asian Americans are fast-growing minority groups. More than 4 percent of Michigan's population is made up of people of Hispanic descent. The Michigan Commission on Spanish-Speaking Affairs was created in 1995 to encourage education about and celebration of Hispanic culture and language, as well as to provide services to the Spanish-speaking community. Each year from September 15 to October 15, Michiganders celebrate Hispanic Heritage Month. Festivities include music, art displays, literary readings, food, and dancing.

People of Asian Indian ancestry make up the largest group of Asian Americans in Michigan. They accounted for more than 30 percent of the state's Asian Americans according to a 2008 estimate by the Census Bureau. Chinese Americans made up the second-largest group, accounting for nearly 19 percent of Asian Americans. Korean Americans were the third-largest group, at about 10 percent. Michigan is home to more than 21,000 businesses that are owned by Asian Americans.

American Indians

American Indians used to make up the entire population of the region. With the arrival of Europeans and then American settlers, however, their numbers decreased. Today, they represent one of the smallest minority groups in the state.

Some of Michigan's American Indians live in towns and cities alongside other Michiganders. They work in the same industries, hold government offices, and attend the local schools. Other American Indian Michiganders live on the various reservations spread across the state. Indian reservations in Michigan include the Bay Mills (Ojibwe), Grand Traverse (Ottawa and Ojibwe), Hannahville (Potawatomi), Huron Potawatomi, Isabella (Ojibwe), Lac Vieux Desert (Ojibwe), L'Anse (Ojibwe), Pokagon (Potawatomi), and Sault Sainte Marie (Ojibwe). Many Indians in the state embrace modern life but also continue to practice the traditions of their ancestors. These traditions are also shared with others through museums, presentations, and powwows and other festivals.

A powwow in Port Huron is an opportunity to celebrate American Indian traditions and culture.

City Life

In the early 1900s, immigrants from all over the world came to Michigan. The state's mills and factories brought the promise of work. Struggling families from other areas of the United States came to Michigan during this time as well, hoping for high-paying jobs.

As manufacturing industries became increasingly important in Michigan's economy, the population in Michigan shifted from farms to cities. In 1850, almost all Michiganders lived in rural areas. But the population of towns and cities was rising, and it continued to rise in the following decades. Then, when the United States entered World War I in 1917, the demands on Michigan's automobile industry grew immensely. The military needed armored vehicles, trucks, and other materials. People moved from the farms of Michigan and from elsewhere in the country to work in the city factories to help meet this demand.

The city of Detroit is the center of a metropolitan area in which almost 45 percent of Michiganders live.

World War I ended in 1918. A little more than a decade later, the Great Depression had a major impact on Michiganders. Because few Americans could afford to buy cars, many automobile workers lost their jobs. By 1933, Michigan's unemployment level reached 46 percent, while the national rate stood at 24 percent. Because of the high cost of farming materials—at a time when farmers were getting very low prices for what they produced—many Michiganders stayed in the cities. Others who had been living on farms joined them.

On a bright summer day, people enjoy the annual art fair in Ann Arbor.

This move to the city has lasted. Today, four-fifths of all Michiganders live in a city or town. The city of Detroit has more people than any other city in Michigan. In 2009, it had an estimated population of more than 900,000, making it the eleventh most populated city in the United States. More than 4.4 million people lived in the Detroit metropolitan area.

Looking to the Future

The population of Michigan grew by almost 7 percent between 1990 and 2000. The following decade saw growth only in some years because the state's economy faced challenges and good jobs were harder to find. Overall, the population of Michigan declined slightly (by less than 1 percent) between 2000 and 2010. But as it has throughout its history, Michigan continues to delight old and new residents alike. The diverse face of cities like Detroit, the beauty of the state's landscapes, and the variety of ways for people to work, play, and enjoy their lives all make Michigan an exciting and enriching place to live.

Calendar of Events

★ Plymouth Ice Festival

Each January, Plymouth celebrates winter with a three-day festival. The Plymouth Ice Festival is best known as one of the largest ice sculpture events in the country. Carvers from around the world come to make art out of great blocks of ice. The festival also features competitions, live music and entertainment, interactive family shows, and food.

★ Michigan Week

Each year in May, state residents celebrate Michigan Week. For seven days, the people of Michigan celebrate their heritage and focus on the traditions that make Michigan special. An annual tradition since 1954, Michigan Week gives the people of the state an opportunity to celebrate culture, tourism, natural resources, educational opportunities, and much more.

★ Tulip Time Festival

Also in May, Holland, Michigan, holds its Tulip Time Festival. In addition to stunning beds of tulips and other flowers, the eight-day festival features parades, special guests, *klompen* dancing (a form of traditional Dutch wooden shoe dancing), music, art exhibits, and food. First held in 1929, the festival is scheduled to coincide with the blossoming of hundreds of thousands of tulips.

★ National Cherry Festival

In July, the Lake Michigan shoreline in Traverse City is home to the National Cherry Festival. The festivities include pie-eating contests, air shows, music and art events, parades, marching bands, and rides. At the end of the weeklong festival, the National Cherry Queen is named.

★ Upper Peninsula State Fair

Escanaba hosts the annual Upper Peninsula State Fair in August. Attractions include agricultural exhibits and competitions, carnival rides, concerts, and auto racing.

★ Old Town BluesFest

Lansing celebrates blues music each September with the Old Town BluesFest, showcasing exceptional local, regional, and national blues musicians. The two-day festival takes place in the city's Old Town neighborhood. In addition to its musical treats, the festival offers visitors a chance to experience the historic area's riverside restaurants, boutiques, and art galleries.

How the Government Works

Government leaders in Michigan need to balance the interests of big businesses and labor unions, of rural farmers and people who live in cities. Serving the interests of all residents is a large job. Lansing is the capital of Michigan, and this is where Michigan's state government is based. There are also many local governments within Michigan.

Local Government

There are eighty-three counties in Michigan. Each county is governed by a board of commissioners. Members of the board are elected by voters in the county for two-year terms, without any limit on the number of terms. The board of commissioners is responsible for making policies that relate to the entire county.

> ### In Their Own Words
>
> *All political power is inherent in the people. Government is instituted for their equal benefit, security, and protection.*
>
> —Article 1, Section 1 of Michigan's constitution

Each county is divided into townships and cities. Cities have home rule. This means they have more freedom in conducting their business than do townships. There also are villages, which have some of the powers of cities but remain a part of a township. As of 2009, Michigan had more

Michigan's governor and legislature work in the Capitol Building in Lansing. The building was completed in 1879.

than 1,200 townships. It also had about 275 cities and nearly 260 villages. Each township, city, and village has its own government. Townships are run by a board of five to seven members. Some cities are governed by an elected council, which appoints a manager to run day-to-day affairs. Other cities are governed by a council and a mayor, who may be directly elected by voters or chosen by the council, generally from among its members. Villages usually are governed by an elected council and president.

State Government

The Michigan state government has three branches: executive, legislative, and judicial. Each branch has its own powers and responsibilities. The executive branch is headed by the governor. The legislative branch is the lawmaking body. The legislature, responsible for passing laws, is made up of two parts, or chambers: the house of representatives and the senate. The judicial branch consists of the courts and related agencies.

An elected state board of education oversees Michigan's schools. It appoints a superintendent of public instruction, who heads the state department of education.

The structure and powers of Michigan's government are set by the state constitution. The current constitution was adopted in 1963. It begins with a declaration of the rights belonging to the people. Several portions of the 1963 constitution have been amended, or changed, over the years.

The floor of the Capitol Building's rotunda, beneath the dome, is made of almost a thousand pieces of thick glass.

Branches of Government

EXECUTIVE ★ ★ ★ ★ ★ ★ ★ ★

Michiganders elect a governor every four years to head the executive branch. They also elect a lieutenant governor, secretary of state, and attorney general. A lifetime limit of two terms in office applies to these four positions. The governor is in charge of appointing important state officials, including most department heads, such as the state treasurer. The governor also appoints hundreds of people to boards and committees, signs bills into law, and plans the state budget. In addition, he or she can call on the state militia to deal with a state emergency. The lieutenant governor presides over the state senate and acts for the governor in the governor's absence. The secretary of state's duties include management of voter registration, driver licensing, and vehicle registration.

LEGISLATIVE ★ ★ ★ ★ ★ ★ ★ ★

The legislative branch of Michigan's government is divided into two parts: the senate and the house of representatives. Michigan has thirty-eight senators, who are elected to four-year terms. A senator can serve no more than two terms. The senate is responsible for approving appointments made by the governor. The Michigan house of representatives is composed of 110 representatives, who are elected to two-year terms. A representative may serve no more than three terms. The legislature is responsible for passing laws, levying taxes, and overseeing the work of the executive branch.

JUDICIAL ★ ★ ★ ★ ★ ★ ★ ★ ★

Michigan's judicial branch is responsible for interpreting laws and trying cases. The highest court is the state supreme court, which is made up of seven justices. Ranking below the supreme court is the court of appeals. Michigan is divided into four districts, each of which elects seven appeals judges. The court of appeals and supreme court generally hear appeals of cases that start in a lower court; in an appeal, one side in a case asks a higher court to review the decision that was made in the lower court and determine whether it was fair and in keeping with the law. There are also fifty-seven circuit courts throughout Michigan, and most counties have probate courts that handle wills and guardianships over individuals. More than one hundred district courts handle many types of criminal and other cases. All the judges in Michigan, other than the state supreme court justices and municipal judges, are elected to six-year terms. Supreme court justices are elected to eight-year terms, and municipal judges to four-year terms. There is no limit on the number of terms that judges can serve.

How a Bill Becomes a Law

When citizens and politicians decide a new law should be made, a bill must be introduced in one of the legislature's chambers. A senator or representative writes the bill, which includes all of the details of the new law being proposed. When a bill is introduced, its title is read. This is the first of three "readings" a bill ordinarily has to go through in each chamber in order to be approved.

Next, the bill is sent to an appropriate committee for discussion. Committees are made up of legislators who have an interest in a certain area. Committees have the power to recommend the bill either in its original form or with amendments. If the bill receives the committee's recommendation, it goes back to the chamber for a second reading. More amendments may be made to the bill at this time. If the bill gains approval to go on to a third reading, the legislators will again vote on the bill. They may decide to make additional amendments. If the bill wins the approval of a majority of the chamber's elected members (for certain types of measures a majority of two-thirds or more is required), it goes to the other chamber of the legislature, and the process is repeated.

If a bill is passed with the same wording in both the senate and the house of representatives, it is sent to the governor. Sometimes, however, the second chamber approves a bill only after changing it. If that happens, the bill then goes back to the first chamber. The first chamber may either accept or reject the new wording. If it accepts the bill in its new form, the bill is sent to the governor. If the first chamber does not accept the new wording, the bill is sent to a conference committee. This committee, consisting of a few members from

Michigan's house of representatives convenes in this room within the Capitol Building.

each chamber, tries to come up with compromise wording acceptable to both chambers.

Once the governor receives a final bill, he or she can sign it, and it becomes a new law. The governor also has the power to veto, or reject, a bill. A bill that the governor disapproves of and vetoes can still become a law, but only if the two legislative chambers vote to override (overrule) the veto. For this to happen, two-thirds of the members of each chamber must vote to override.

Contacting Lawmakers

★ ★ ★ ★ ★ ★ ★ ★ ★ ★ ★ ★

To find out how to get in touch with Michigan legislators, go to this website:

http://www.legislature.mi.gov

By following the links on the site, you will be able to learn who represents each district in Michigan. Click on "Contact your Representative" to find the names and contact information for members of the house of representatives. Click on "Contact your Senator" to learn the names of members of the senate.

Getting Involved

The job of every Michigan politician is to represent the voice of the people. But Michiganders must speak their minds in order for their representatives to work on their behalf. You can share your opinions with your local representatives. Write a letter or send an e-mail to your representatives. Let them know how you feel about the issues that are important to you.

Quick Facts

MICHIGANDERS IN CONGRESS

Like all states, Michigan elects two senators to the U.S. Senate. The number of members each state has in the U.S. House of Representatives is related to the state's population and can change after each U.S. Census is taken. Based on results of the 2010 Census, Michigan will have 14 representatives beginning in 2013, one less than it had for the previous decade.

Making a Living

Michigan is home to many different types of industries, including tourism, manufacturing, and farming. The state has weathered many ups and downs in the economy, but it has always found a way to recover.

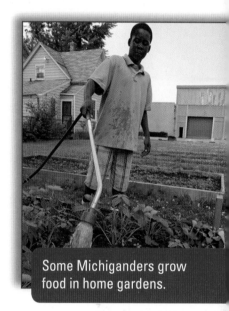
Some Michiganders grow food in home gardens.

Agriculture

Michigan has been ideal for agriculture since Indians first began farming the land centuries ago. As of 2009, there were about 54,800 farms in Michigan. The state leads the United States in the production of such crops as blueberries, tart cherries, cucumbers for pickles, and squash. Other crops for which Michigan ranks among the leading states include apples, asparagus, beans, grapes, potatoes, and sugar beets. Corn, soybeans, wheat, sugar beets, and potatoes are the crops that bring in the most money for the state's farmers.

The farms of Michigan are not just for growing crops. Some are livestock farms, where cattle, pigs, sheep, and lambs are raised. Michigan's turkey farms raised more than 5 million turkeys in 2007. Milk is one of Michigan's biggest farm products. In 2009, Michigan cows produced 8 billion pounds (3.6 billion kg) of milk, which made up 4.2 percent of total U.S. milk production.

Vehicles roll down an assembly line at the huge Ford Rouge Center plant south of Detroit.

RECIPE FOR CHERRY CREAM PIE

Cherries are a major crop in Michigan. Here is a recipe that uses this delicious fruit.

WHAT YOU NEED

12-ounce package (340 grams) vanilla wafers

1 cup (250 g) whipping cream

8-ounce package (225 g) cream cheese, softened

$1/2$ cup (50 g) confectioners' sugar

21-ounce can (595 g) cherry pie filling

Crumble the vanilla wafers into a 9-inch x 9-inch (23-cm x 23-cm) pan and set the pan aside.

In a medium-sized bowl, whip the cream. Set the whipped cream aside.

In a separate mixing bowl, whip together the cream cheese and the confectioners' sugar until the mixture is smooth and fluffy. If you have problems mixing these things, you can ask an adult to help.

Mix the whipped cream into the cream cheese mixture. Spoon this over the crumbled wafer cookies.

Spread the cherry pie filling evenly over the top of the mixture. If you like, you can crumble a few extra wafers and spread that over the pie filling.

Cover the pan and refrigerate it overnight. Then, scoop out a piece and enjoy.

A freighter approaches an iron ore loading dock at Marquette, on the shore of Lake Superior in the Upper Peninsula.

Mining

Michigan has a long history of mining, especially in the Upper Peninsula. Some of the minerals found naturally in Michigan include copper, iron, gold, silver, gypsum, slate, salt, coal, and limestone.

Iron ore was mined heavily beginning in the mid-1800s. Iron deposits were found in Marquette, Menominee, and Gogebic counties in the western half of the Upper Peninsula. But very little high-grade iron ore remains in Michigan.

High-grade iron ore has a high proportion of iron. Low-grade iron ore has some iron in it, but it also has high levels of other minerals. A low-grade ore called taconite is still mined in Michigan's Upper Peninsula. Michigan supplied about 23 percent of the iron ore produced in the United States in 2008. This iron is mostly used to make steel, which in turn is used for such things as making cars and constructing bridges and buildings.

Copper mining in Michigan began long ago when Indians used simple tools to dig for the metal. Between 1847 and 1887, Michigan was the top copper producer in the United States. Copper was mined into the twentieth century. But the state's copper resources were decreasing, and in 1995, the last big copper mine in Michigan closed.

Forestry

Forestry has been an important industry for Michigan. Lumber and wood products contribute billions of dollars to Michigan's economy each year. Unlike minerals that were mined almost until they disappeared, trees are a renewable resource if they are forested responsibly. As trees are cut down for lumber, paper, and other products, new trees can be planted in their place.

The forestry industry went into full swing in the 1840s. White pine—a wood often used to make buildings—was plentiful in the Upper Peninsula. Without

Quick Facts

STATE SOIL
Soil is an important factor in both farming and forestry. There are hundreds of different types of soils in Michigan. In 1990, Michigan lawmakers picked one of them, Kalkaska sand, as the official state soil. First described in 1927 in Kalkaska County, it is found only in Michigan and occurs in more than a third of the state's counties. Trees such as sugar maple and yellow birch grow on Kalkaska sand, as do crops such as potatoes and strawberries. The soil is important in Christmas tree production and also is found in wildlife habitat areas and recreation areas.

Workers & Industries

Industry	Number of People Working in That Industry	Percentage of All Workers Who Are Working in That Industry
Education and health care	1,036,241	22.7%
Manufacturing	824,807	18.1%
Wholesale and retail businesses	663,658	14.5%
Publishing, media, entertainment, hotels, and restaurants	501,074	11.0%
Professionals, scientists, and managers	419,160	9.2%
Banking and finance, insurance, and real estate	257,483	5.6%
Construction	237,503	5.2%
Other services	212,609	4.7%
Transportation and public utilities	197,484	4.3%
Government	161,868	3.5%
Farming, fishing, forestry, and mining	56,365	1.2%
Totals	**4,568,252**	**100%**

Notes: Figures above do not include people in the armed forces. "Professionals" includes people such as doctors and lawyers. Percentages may not add to 100 because of rounding.

Source: U.S. Bureau of the Census, 2008 estimates

trucks to help move wood to other areas, a network of streams, rivers, and canals was used to transport lumber. The huge pieces of wood could be placed on a barge and floated downstream to sawmills and ports. From 1869 to the end of the nineteenth century, Michigan produced more lumber than any other state.

With so much wood available, Michiganders began crafting beautiful furniture. Grand Rapids earned fame as the furniture capital of the world in the late nineteenth century. Today, it still claims the title of office furniture capital of the world.

Manufacturing

Michigan is often associated with the automobile industry. The Detroit area is known as the automotive capital of the United States. Since the early 1900s, Michigan has played an important role in the making of cars. Ford Motor Company, headquartered in Dearborn, was founded in 1903. General Motors began in Flint in 1908 and is now based in Detroit. Chrysler started making cars in Michigan in 1925 and is based in the Detroit suburb of Auburn Hills. In 2007, Michigan accounted for about one-fourth of all the cars that were made in the United States.

Michigan manufactures a lot of other products as well. Kellogg, known for its breakfast cereals, was founded in Battle Creek, where its headquarters are still located. Post, another major breakfast cereal maker, also began in Battle Creek and still has manufacturing facilities there. Gerber, the leading maker of baby food in the United States, sells baby food from Michigan to parents all over the world. Other products made in Michigan include machinery, furniture, appliances, chemicals, and pharmaceuticals. Hundreds of thousands of Michiganders work in manufacturing these and other products.

Gerber's baby food plant is a major employer in the Fremont area.

Celery

Celery was first brought to Michigan in the 1850s from Scotland. The wet soil of the Kalamazoo swamps—located at the bottom of the Lower Peninsula—is ideal for growing celery, which requires dark, moist soil called muck. Today, Michigan produces more celery than any other state except California.

Christmas Trees

Michigan ranks among the top states producing Christmas trees. The Scotch pine and Douglas fir varieties are among the most popular Christmas trees grown in Michigan. In fact, Christmas trees are among the state's top-twenty most valuable crops. Christmas tree farmers in Michigan harvest more than one million trees each year.

Iron

Although most of the best iron ore was mined in the 1800s, Michigan is still a major source for iron. Iron from Michigan finds its way into buildings, bridges, and many other structures all across the United States.

Asparagus

Michigan ranks third in the United States for asparagus production. Asparagus thrives in the soil near the shores of Lake Michigan. Many growers boast that only Michigan asparagus is hand-snapped above the ground, which makes for more tender and flavorful asparagus.

Tourism

With attractions like Mackinac Island, the blues clubs of Detroit, more than 115 lighthouses, gorgeous waterfalls, amazing sand dunes, and the coasts of four Great Lakes, Michigan is a popular place to visit. More than 150,000 Michiganders work in a tourism-related industry. Travelers spend more than $15 billion in Michigan each year, giving a healthy boost to the state's economy.

Cranberries

Cranberries grow on vines, usually in sandy soil in wetlands. Michigan's wetland areas are ideal for planting cranberries. Michigan has roughly 250 acres (100 ha) of cranberry bogs. The cranberries are sold fresh or dried, or are made into products that are sent across the state and around the country.

Tourism and Services

With its many freshwater lakes and rivers, sand dunes, and shorelines, Michigan is a popular place to visit. The tourism industry makes $15 billion per year. It also provides many jobs for the people of Michigan. Some popular places in Michigan to visit include the Henry Ford Museum and Greenfield Village in Dearborn, the Capitol Building in Lansing, the Sleeping Bear Sand Dunes National Lakeshore, the Straits of Mackinac, the Mackinac Bridge, Mackinac Island, the Porcupine Mountains Wilderness State Park, and Tahquamenon Falls.

Summer remains one of the most popular times to visit Michigan. Tourists come to sail the waters of the Great Lakes, enjoy the warm weather, and visit the many natural landmarks Michigan has to offer, such as the sand dunes, beaches, and forests. Spring is a popular time for trout and bass fishing. In the winter months, visitors ski, snowmobile, ice fish, and ice-skate. Fall is a beautiful time to drive the hills of Michigan and admire the changing leaves of Michigan's forests.

There are many museums in Michigan. Some explore different aspects of Michigan's rich history. The Public Museum in Grand Rapids is home to a permanent exhibition called Furniture City, which celebrates the state's furniture-making heritage. The Michigan Historical Museum in Lansing brings the history of Michigan alive in its "First People" exhibit. There also are notable art museums, with the Detroit Institute of Arts ranking as the biggest.

Sporting events also bring money to the state. Detroit has four major professional sports teams: the Tigers in baseball, the Pistons in basketball, the Lions in football, and the Red Wings in hockey. Residents from around the state and visitors from across the country come to the city to attend games. The money spent on tickets, souvenirs, food, hotel expenses, and other purchases helps the state's and the city's economy.

Many music lovers come to Michigan to see the Motown Historical Museum in Detroit or to hear the Detroit Symphony Orchestra. Thrill-seekers visit Mackinaw City to go parasailing over the waters of Lake Huron. Mackinaw City also offers a chance to work through a life-sized maze of mirrors, as does

The University of Michigan's stadium in Ann Arbor can hold 72,000 football fans.

Frankenmuth's Ultimate Mirror Maze. Whether tourists seek an outdoor, a cultural, or a learning experience, Michigan is a place to find it all.

The tourism industry is a part of the larger service industry. The service industry includes any jobs that provide a service to others. The people who work in stores, sell souvenirs, and manage hotels and restaurants are all a part of the service industry. Bankers, doctors, nurses, insurance agents, and tour guides are also part of the service industry and play an important part in the state's economy. So do teachers. Besides those who work in schools, a large number have jobs at Michigan's many colleges and universities, which also employ scientists and other people in the service industry. The state's two largest public universities are Michigan State University, at East Lansing, and the University of Michigan, which has its main campus in Ann Arbor and branch campuses at Dearborn and Flint.

Preserving the natural environment, and the animals that live within it, is important to the people of Michigan.

Protecting the Environment

The state has always depended on the land and its natural resources. Because of this, protecting the natural environment is important to the state. It is so important, in fact, that the Michigan government has worked to educate people about what they can do to keep Michigan clean. Like a number of other states, Michigan takes part in the federally sponsored Conservation Reserve Enhancement Program, which is designed to encourage farmers to help protect soil and water quality and wildlife habitats. Michigan's efforts in this program have focused on the Lake Macatawa, River Raisin, and Saginaw Bay regions. The Michigan Groundwater Stewardship Program aims to prevent fertilizer from contaminating Michigan's groundwater (naturally occurring underground supplies of fresh water).

Michigan also has an extensive recycling plan. But it does even more than recycle newspapers, aluminum cans, and plastics. In 1995, it became the first state to start a recycling program for empty aerosol cans, which has helped the environment. In 1993, Michigan began recycling plastic pesticide containers to help maintain the quality of groundwater.

By paying attention to their environment, Michiganders show how deeply they care about their state. Through conservation efforts, they are trying to make sure that the people of the state will always be able to enjoy the beautiful land that Michigan is today.

State Flag & Seal

The Michigan state flag was adopted in 1911. It is a blue flag with the Michigan coat of arms in the middle. Near the top of the state coat of arms is a bald eagle holding arrows and an olive branch, a symbol of peace. The moose and elk are symbols of Michigan, and they are supporting a shield with a man standing on a grassy peninsula. The man's right hand is raised in peace, and his left hand holds a gun, indicating his willingness to defend the state and the nation. There are three Latin sayings on the coat of arms: "E Pluribus Unum" which means "from many, one." This refers to the many states that make up the United States. "Tuebor" means "I will defend." "Si Quaeris Peninsulam Amoenam Circumspice" is the state motto, and it means, "If you seek a pleasant peninsula, look about you."

Michigan's state seal shows the state coat of arms encircled by the words "The Great Seal of the State of Michigan A.D. MDCCCXXXV," which in Roman numerals stands for 1835, the year the seal was adopted.

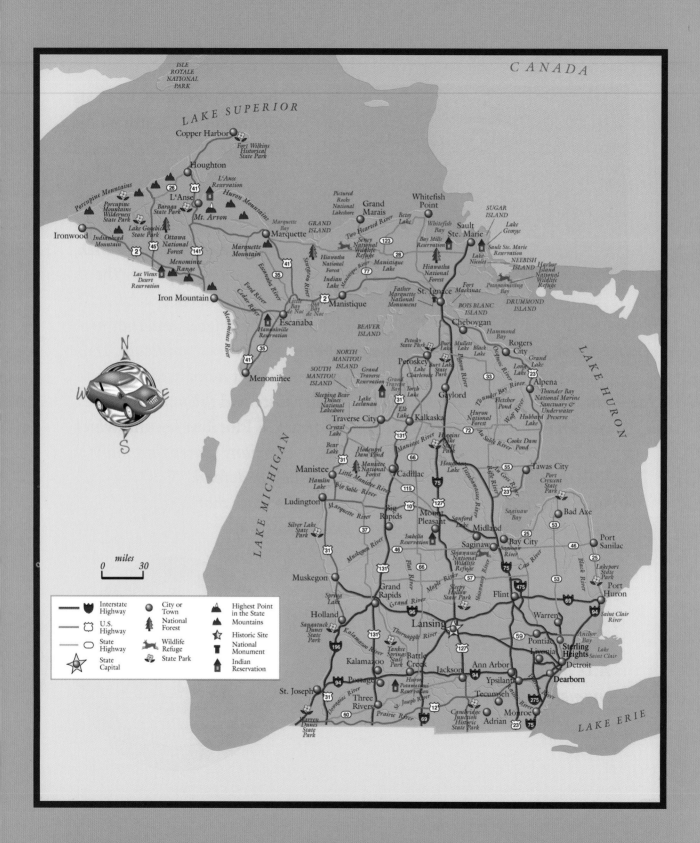

CANADA

ISLE ROYALE NATIONAL PARK

LAKE SUPERIOR

Copper Harbor
Fort Wilkins Historical State Park

Houghton

L'Anse Reservation

L'Anse
Baraga State Park
Mt. Arvon

Huron Mountains

Porcupine Mountains

Porcupine Mountains Wilderness State Park
Lake Gogebic State Park

Ironwood
Indianhead Mountain
Ottawa National Forest

Menominee Range

Lac Vieux Desert Reservation

Iron Mountain

Marquette Bay

GRAND ISLAND

Pictured Rocks National Lakeshore

Grand Marais

Betsy Lake

Whitefish Point

Whitefish Bay

SUGAR ISLAND

Lake George

Sault Ste. Marie

Bay Mills Reservation
Sault Ste. Marie Reservation

Two Hearted River
Seney National Wildlife Refuge

Hiawatha National Forest

Manistique Lake

Lake Nicolet

NEEBISH ISLAND

Harbor Island National Wildlife Refuge

141

Marquette

35

Marquette Mountain

Escanaba River
Cedar River

Sturgeon River

Little Bay de Noc
Big Bay de Noc

77

Indian Lake

Manistique

2

Father Marquette National Monument

St. Ignace

Hiawatha National Forest

Fort Mackinac

Potagannissing Bay

BOIS BLANC ISLAND

DRUMMOND ISLAND

Hauntville Reservation

Escanaba

35

41

Menominee

NORTH MANITOU ISLAND

SOUTH MANITOU ISLAND

BEAVER ISLAND

Cheboygan

Hammond Bay

Petosky State Park

Burt Lake
Mullett Lake
Black Lake

Rogers City

Ocqueoc River

Grand Lake
Long Lake

23

Grand Traverse Reservation

Sleeping Bear Dunes National Lakeshore

Lake Leelanau

Grand Traverse Bay

Petoskey

Burt Lake State Park

Lake Charlevoix

Torch Lake

Pigeon River

Gaylord

33

Thunder Bay River

Alpena

Thunder Bay National Marine Sanctuary & Underwater Preserve

Traverse City

Crystal Lake

Elk Lake

Kalkaska

31

Au Sable River

72

Huron National Forest

Fletcher Pond
Wolf River
Hubbard Lake

Cooke Dam Pond

Bear Lake

Hodenpyl Dam Pond

Manistee River

Higgins Lake
Higgins Lake State Park

Houghton Lake

55

Au Gres River

Tawas City

Port Crescent State Park

Manistee

131

Little Manistee River

Manistee National Forest

Cadillac

66

Tittabawassee River

Bad Axe

53

Hamlin Lake

115

10

Big Rapids

127

75

Mount Pleasant

Sanford Lake

Midland

25

Saginaw Bay

Port Sanilac

Ludington

Silver Lake State Park

Marquette River

Big Sable River

37

Muskegon River

46

Isabella Reservation

Shiawassee National Wildlife Refuge

Saginaw

Saginaw River

Cass River

Bay City

75

Black River

Lakeport State Park

53

46

25

Muskegon

Spring Lake

131

Flat River

66

Maple River

57

Sleepy Hollow State Park

Flint

475

69

Port Huron

94

Saint Clair River

Anchor Bay

Grand Rapids

Grand River

Holland

96

Saugatuck Dunes State Park

Thornapple River

Lansing

127

Warren

59

Pontiac

Livonia

Sterling Heights

Detroit

Lake Saint Clair

196

Kalamazoo

Yankee Springs State Park

Battle Creek

Kalamazoo River

Jackson

94

Ann Arbor

Ypsilanti

Tecumseh

275

Dearborn

St. Joseph

31

Portage

Huron Potawatomi Reservation

Three Rivers

60

Dowagiac River

St. Joseph River

Prairie River

69

12

Cambridge Junction Historic State Park

Monroe

Adrian

23

75

Warren Dunes State Park

LAKE MICHIGAN

LAKE HURON

LAKE ERIE

miles
0   30

N
W   E
S

Interstate Highway
U.S. Highway
State Highway
State Capital

City or Town
National Forest
Wildlife Refuge
State Park

Highest Point in the State
Mountains
Historic Site
National Monument
Indian Reservation

State Song

Michigan, My Michigan

words by Douglas Malloch
sung to the tune of "O Christmas Tree"

A song to thee, fair State of mine, Mich – i-gan, my Mich-i-gan; But

great – er song than this is thine, Mich – i – gan, my Mich – i-gan; The

whis-per of the for – est tree, The thun-der of the in-land sea, U – nite in

one grand sym – pho – ny Of Mich – i-gan, my Mich – i – gan.

BOOKS

Domm, Robert W. *Michigan Yesterday & Today*. Minneapolis, MN: Voyageur Press, 2009.

Godfrey, Linda S. *Weird Michigan: Your Travel Guide to Michigan's Local Legends and Best Kept Secrets*. New York: Sterling, 2006.

Martone, Laura. *Moon Michigan*. Berkeley, CA: Avalon Travel, 2009.

Sobczak, John. *A Motor City Year*. Detroit: Wayne State University Press, 2009.

Vachon, Paul. *Forgotten Detroit*. Charleston, SC: Arcadia, 2009.

WEBSITES

Michigan Photographs
http://www.h-net.org/~michigan/photos/index.html

Official State of Michigan website
http://www.michigan.gov

Pure Michigan: Michigan's Official Travel and Tourism Site
http://travel.michigan.org

Seeking Michigan
http://seekingmichigan.org

Johannah Haney writes books and magazine articles in Boston, Massachusetts. Growing up, she often visited family in Michigan from her hometown in Ohio, which is on Michigan's southern border.

Richard Hantula is a writer and editor. Born and brought up in Michigan, he now lives in New York City.

Page numbers in **boldface** are illustrations.